Singing with Jesus

Singing with Jesus

The Lord's Psalm

KURT C. SCHAEFER

WIPF & STOCK · Eugene, Oregon

SINGING WITH JESUS
The Lord's Psalm

Copyright © 2018 Kurt C. Schaefer. All rights reserved. Except for brief quotations in critical publications or reviews, no part of this book may be reproduced in any manner without prior written permission from the publisher. Write: Permissions, Wipf and Stock Publishers, 199 W. 8th Ave., Suite 3, Eugene, OR 97401.

Wipf & Stock
An Imprint of Wipf and Stock Publishers
199 W. 8th Ave., Suite 3
Eugene, OR 97401

www.wipfandstock.com

PAPERBACK ISBN: 978-1-5326-4682-9
HARDCOVER ISBN: 978-1-5326-4683-6
EBOOK ISBN: 978-1-5326-4684-3

Manufactured in the U.S.A.

Scripture quotations are from New Revised Standard Version Bible, copyright © 1989 National Council of the Churches of Christ in the United States of America. Used by permission. All rights reserved worldwide.

For Wilbur Carls Schaefer, who lived the orderly sort of life in which everything begins to resemble prayer.

Contents

Preface | ix

Chapter 1: What Makes Hebrew Poetry Poetic? | 1

Chapter 2: Selections from Jesus' Prayer Book | 12

Chapter 3: The Prayer of Our Lord | 35

Appendix: Field Guide to Hebrew Poetry | 55

Preface

When the disciples asked Jesus how to pray, he responded by writing a psalm.

The psalms were the default prayer book of Jesus' culture, and the disciples sang psalms together (on the way to Gethsemane, for example). So yes, of course, Jesus would probably write his great prayer for disciples as a psalm. And, as we will see, the Lord's Prayer certainly is, in its form, a Hebrew poem—a psalm.

Psalms communicate their truth and beauty in particular ways. For the disciples, these conventions of Hebrew poetry were probably second nature. For us, not so much. We are liable to miss some of the important things that Jesus was teaching in this prayer, because writing communicates, in part, through its forms, not just its words.

So this book is about the Lord's Prayer, but it's also about how to read the Bible well—in particular, how to read, understand, and love Hebrew poetry. It's a book about noticing beauty. When I began to learn (in seminary) about reading Hebrew poetry, I started to feel that I had been missing a lot. I'd faithfully attended church and Sunday School for over fifty years, but I didn't know much about how to read the many Bible texts that are poetic. It felt like I'd been studying Shakespeare for fifty years without understanding what "thou" means. So you could think of this little book as a short course in a rich and rewarding topic. It should make much of your Bible reading more deeply engaging.

Preface

I do think it may be best to approach this book as a *course*. It's not that learning to love Hebrew poetry is very hard, but it's probably not light beach reading, either. I suppose it's like learning to crochet or ride a bike: You learn a few simple rules, and then you practice a while, and suddenly you know how to do it. A new world has opened up before you.

The main difficulty may be allowing the beauty in front of you to be appreciated. If you're like me—from a place heavily influenced by Europe—you grew up in a culture that for centuries has believed in its own superiority. Those poor, backward people who lived before *we* arrived were dull and superstitious, right? So when we see that they produced and understood very advanced literature, beauty so sly that *we* hadn't noticed it, we're likely to react with a "No, no, this can't be; those peasants were not capable of this." It's true that modern culture has made some technical innovations that are unprecedented, but that's largely because we've focused our work and institutions on technology and become quite specialized—narrow, that is—in our professions. Prior cultures were not less intelligent, and they seem to have given more of their energy to things like literature. It may take some humility to admit that some of their elegance escapes us until we give it focused attention.

This little book is a printed, expanded version of some talks I gave to college students in the fall of 2012 and a church adult-education series in January of 2013. I worked with the same materials in a few more adult-education classes and college chapel sermons in the winter and spring of 2015. Several people commented that they wished the classes and talks were available in book form. So you could also think of this book as a series of chats among people who pray.

I'm grateful to my seminary professors who helped me to love the languages and poetry of the Bible. They maintained a curriculum heavy on Hebrew and Greek, even though so many seminaries have departed from that tradition. In my case this was a wonderful gift. All of the analysis here, except for the parts that are widely available in many textbooks and other places, is original

Preface

so far as I know, so we shouldn't fault my professors or others for mistakes I make here.

I'm especially grateful to the parishioners and college students who helped me to think more clearly as we studied this material together. Thanks for being my teachers.

I am in debt to Wilbur Schaefer, whose comments significantly improved the tone of what you will find here, and to Lois Nordling for her thoughtful comments on a full draft. My conversations with David Suryk about N. T. Wright's books have also flavored what you will find here. And I was very happy to recently see David Clark's new book on the Lord's Prayer, which helpfully confirmed some parts of this work.

I am particularly thankful to the New York Public Library's Stephen A. Schwarzman Building for taking me in as a researcher-in-residence to work on this project. My work also heavily depended on the Manhattan Research Library Initiative, which granted generous access to the research holdings at Columbia University, Union Theological Seminary, and New York University. My SEO scholars at the Manhattan Leadership and Public Service High School, and my math scholars at Mustard Seed School in Hoboken, New Jersey, really helped me to live out the conviction that serious scholarship can also be fun to read and accessible to people of all ages.

Most of all, I am grateful for Anne, who has walked with me for nearly forty years, taught me to be a reader, and provided for us while I worked on this book. If you have the pleasure of knowing her, I'm sure you'll recognize her influence as you read.

Please be in touch if you'd like to talk more about the things you will find in this book.

Grand Rapids, Michigan
December 24, 2017

Chapter One

What Makes Hebrew Poetry Poetic?

SERIOUSLY? I MEAN—*SERIOUSLY?!?* DO we really need *another* book about the Lord's Prayer?

Well, think about what you're doing right now. How do you make sense of this book—in fact, of anything that is written down?

- You have to understand the meaning of each *word*, of course.

- You need to know enough *grammar* to reconstruct the intention of the words as grouped into sentences.

- You have to pin together the ideas in the sentences to discover the structure of logic running through *paragraphs*.

- You have to understand the *genre*—the type of writing—because you read the words, sentences, and paragraphs of newspaper reports differently than you read satire or poetry or campaign speeches. You might call this the *aesthetic context* of the writing.

- You will also miss a lot if you don't know something about the context of this writing among other similar writings in its genre. Call this the *literary context*.

- You're liable to go very wrong if you don't know the *historical and cultural context* of the writing; often that context redefines the meanings of the individual words and sentences with which you started.

- All of these issues are amplified if you're reading something *in translation* from a different language, which may have a different grammar, different genres, and a different historical and cultural context. This is exactly our situation when we try to pray the Lord's Prayer—probably spoken originally in Aramaic, then written down in the Gospels' *Koine* Greek.

Though we know that translating involves making difficult choices among good alternatives, we trust that the translators have done a good job of bearing witness to the original words and grammar. And perhaps we've read enough books, or heard enough good sermons, to feel we have a sense of the historical and cultural context—at least a good-enough sense—to understand the gist of the prayer.

And yet . . . don't we still have some nagging questions? Like, "Why do we even need to ask God to *not* lead us into temptation?!? Doesn't the Bible say that God never tempts anyone?" Or, "If God is 'our Father who art in heaven,' does that mean God is not present on earth? Isn't God present everywhere?" Or, "What does 'hallowed' mean? I have never used that word in conversation." Or, "Should it be 'debts' or 'trespasses?' If I need to forgive others' debts and trespasses, does that mean I shouldn't take anyone to court for breach-of-contract or breaking-and-entering?"

I think that these questions are related to a different issue, which you could find lurking in the paragraph just before the last one. We may feel we understand this prayer's words, grammar, and historical/cultural context, but how confident are we that we've mastered the prayer's *genre*—that we know what sort of writing this prayer is? If the answer is "not very sure," that's a problem, because genre affects the meanings of words, the implications of grammar, and the literary and cultural context of the writing.

I'd be willing to bet (OK, not really . . . that's a poetic idiom, not a statement of fact) that, if you've read about the Lord's Prayer or heard a sermon about it, you've been told it consists of *seven petitions*. That's a way of identifying the prayer's genre. "Seven petitions" is, in everyday speech, *a list*, a list of requests. The Lord's Prayer has been taught, discussed, and prayed as seven petitions

What Makes Hebrew Poetry Poetic?

(plus an introductory phrase) for a *very* long time, so it's obvious that many people have found this to be a useful way of thinking about the prayer.

On the other hand, . . . the Bible itself never speaks of the Lord's Prayer as a list of seven requests. If that were the only useful way to view this prayer, then a robust understanding of its genre is not going to help us at all, because it's just a list.

When you read through the prayers of the Bible, in the Psalms and elsewhere, you see that prayer is meant to be more than reciting lists of requests. Asking for more things may be our instinctive way of approaching God—"I've done my part, and now it's time for you to pay up"—but that's not the attitude you find in the Scriptures. Prayer is a means of developing relationships—between God and the person praying, and among the community of people who are praying. Prayer sometimes implores, but it also worships; it confesses, and it recounts the history of mercy and covenant that the community has experienced; it rebukes and it encourages; it adores, proclaiming God's importance and beauty; it announces God's mercy and judgment and glory.

You would expect that Jesus' model prayer would do some of these things as well—that it would not just be a list of petitions. He was a person of deep and frequent prayer, and he was a brilliant teacher, literate in Hebrew and Aramaic and, so say many scholars, probably Greek. So when his disciples were ready to learn about prayer, you'd expect Jesus, anticipating that his teaching would inform the entire church, would carefully work out some instruction that is rich in its words, sentences, logic, genre, and literary/historical/cultural references.

You might even say that it seems a little iffy to think of the Lord's Prayer as seven *petitions* when the first three aren't quite requests, really. They are blessings. People like me, of northern European heritage, can easily miss this, because we really don't bless people very often, at least not in the traditional way. But from the Middle East you can easily imagine blessings like "may your son become famous throughout Israel" (Ruth 4:14 NRSV) or "may you be fruitful" (Gen 1:28; 9:7; 24:60; 35:11, and elsewhere) or "may you live to see your children's children" (Ps 128:6). Those blessings are parallel in form to the first three elements in the *Koine* Greek text of the Lord's Prayer: "may your name be hallowed," "may your kingdom come," "may your will be done." (Those are aorist third-person imperatives, passive-active-passive voices, for you *Koine* grammar fans.) The Psalms are often imploring God's people to "bless the Lord," and that's exactly how this prayer starts—with blessings.

The primary prayer book for Jesus and his friends was the book of Psalms. So if Jesus set out to write a prayer that also gives instruction about how to pray, it would be no surprise if he put his teaching in the form of a psalm rather than a list. This is one of the things that great teachers do; they model while they instruct. In fact, as we'll see, this is not the only time Jesus put crucial teaching into the memorable form of a psalm. Doing so was one way of communicating that he is the promised heir of David's royal rule, the son of David the great psalmist. God had repeatedly promised that he would establish a righteous and unending reign in David's line, and Jesus portrays himself as the fulfillment of the Hebrew Scriptures' promised Anointed One—the Messiah, the Christ.

That Anointed One was expected to combine this perpetual righteous *kingdom* with an unending teaching ministry of *prophecy*, and a continuing *priesthood* of mediation between God and the creation. We'll see that Jesus' prayer-psalm, the Lord's Prayer, draws together images of all three of these anointed messianic offices—prophet, priest, and king—by its constant references to the exodus. God's people were awaiting the Messiah, the ultimate prophet, priest, and king, who as the ultimate Moses would enact the ultimate Passover feast, and lead them in the ultimate exodus from the ways of bondage, toward the ultimate promised land. In that land, God's rule would be apparent, and the ancient fracture between heaven and earth would finally be healed. In his prayer Jesus shows himself to be this Messiah, and draws God's people into alignment with this incredible, cosmic work of his.

But we've gotten ahead of ourselves. Why am I so sure that the Lord's Prayer is in the form of a psalm? And how is our

What Makes Hebrew Poetry Poetic?

understanding of the prayer changed by knowing that "psalm" is its genre? To begin answering those questions, we need to explore the things that make Hebrew poetry poetic.

The Poetry of the Psalms . . . and of the Prophets, and the Priests, and the Kings . . .

If you have a Bible handy—preferably not the King James Version, for the purposes of this demonstration—open it to somewhere near the center. You've probably landed in the book of Psalms. What do you notice about the way the words are printed on the page?

> Quickly you will notice,
> > more quickly than I can point out,
> That the words are arranged into paired phrases,
> > One related phrase following the first,
> Twinned phrases that form a single meaning,
> > a joint meaning formed by reiteration, amplification, or contrast.
> Always a first line,
> > a first line followed by a second,
> > the second occasionally followed by an expository third line.
> Rarely, for emphasis, there's a single line.

Hebrew poetry works by using *parallelism*, by creating and exploring meaning across paired phrases that are stacked up into stanzas. It's been pointed out that much of pagan Classical poetry relied upon heroic overstatement, clever turns of phrase, and other linguistic devices, but for Hebrews poetry is generally about relationships—the relationships among words and between paired lines. It's as if Hebrew writing wants to mirror and explore in poetry the relationships embodied in God's covenant relationship with Israel. For Hebrews, being human—being God's people—is all about being in covenant relationship with God and with others. It is *relationship*, not pagan heroism, that lurks in every line.

Of course, when I employed parallelism in my poem just now it didn't prevent me from also trying to write with elegance. "Quickly" comes near the front of the first two lines, to draw in your attention by creating some urgency, and also to make the point that parallelism in Hebrew writing is obvious, once you've noticed it. In the next two pairs of lines "phrase" or "meaning" comes near the end of the first line and is repeated at the beginning of the second, to help draw your eye through the lines, and to help establish the idea of parallel, related lines. "Phrase" is the theme of the second pair, and it also appears near the start of the third pair, to keep some momentum going as you read. "First," "second," and "third" are prominent by repetition when I'm teaching about the occasional three-line phrase; that prominence sets up the contrast of the final, exclamatory, un-paralleled punch line of the psalm. That last line is the exception that proves the rule; it wouldn't have the force of a punch line if most Hebrew poetry weren't written in parallel couples of lines.

And the psalm, taken as a unit, shows that the *form* of writing, the genre, can be a powerful and memorable mechanism for teaching and creating meaning. That, after all, is the main point of this section of this book. I could have just given you all of that information about Hebrew poetry in the form of a list, "Attributes of Hebrew Poetry, and Clever Ways to Supplement Them," but that would be, well, boring. And because it would be boring, you would quickly forget it. Hebrew poetry is *a form* that's powerful in *forming us*; its conventions allow the writer to clarify, reiterate, analyze, exhort, contrast, exclaim, and recollect, all in an artful and memorable way.

Now if you still have an open Bible, start paging toward the end of the book. You'll pass through much of the Hebrew prophetic literature, and you'll notice that a lot of Hebrew prophecy is also written in the form of poetry, similar to the Psalms. In fact, as you page around in the Hebrew Bible you'll begin to notice that a whole lot of it is written in the poetry of parallelism. So learning about Hebrew poetry will help us understand much of the Bible, not just the Lord's Prayer.

What Makes Hebrew Poetry Poetic?

In fact, the poetry of parallelism is so powerful that, once you have noticed it, you'll see it turning up all over. Last Sunday, on the subway to church, the conductor introduced his announcement with a short psalm:

May I please have your attention,
    Ladies and gentlemen?
Ladies and gentlemen,
    May I have your attention, please? . . .

That's parallelism, no doubt about it. (It just goes to show how polite [and poetic] New Yorkers can be [when they feel like it].) This particular little poem is also in a form that we'll see again. People who study such things would call it a *chiasm* (which is a reference to the Greek letter *chi*, an X). In a chiastic psalm, the first idea is echoed in the *last* idea, the second idea echoed in the second-to-last idea, and so forth. If you indent the lines to identify where the echoes are, you get a poem whose left margin looks like an X:

May I please have your attention,
    Ladies and gentlemen?
    Ladies and gentlemen,
May I have your attention, please? . . .

Most people think that chiasms were a form that helped people memorize. This was especially useful in the days when writing materials could be scarce. Chiasms also are a way to communicate ideas artfully; often the emphatic "point" of the poem appears in the middle, at the "point" of the X, with a secondary emphasis coming at the first and last lines of the poem. (Of course, this little poem is so short that it only has a middle and a first/last line combination, but the rule works for longer poems, too.)

And our subway poet used one more device typical of biblical writing: an *inclusio*. The poet signaled the end of a section of the poem by repeating a word that came at the beginning. ("May I please . . . attention, please?") It gives you a mental hint that a section is ending, and was probably particularly helpful in the days when texts were written without punctuation, indentation, or capitalization, and sometimes even without spaces between the words.

A GENRE FOR YOU, TOO

I think that the best way to learn about and appreciate Hebrew poetry is to write some poems. So let's put together a short psalm.

The essence of these poems is parallelism, but you also want the poem to *communicate something*, not just wander around in the dictionary. So I think it's easiest to start by writing *just the first lines* from each pair of lines in the poem. Then you can go back and fill in the second lines, using the type of parallelism that seems best in each case. And then you can dress the whole thing up with some stylistic flourishes.

By most accounts, there are four basic kinds of Hebrew parallelism. For this exercise I'd like to use them all, so let's plan on a four-part psalm—four pairs of phrases.

What should our psalm be about? The Bible's psalms cover a lot of ground. Some are laments, some tell the plot of a story, some are exclamations of praise, some were written for special commemorative occasions (like the coronation of a new king), some portray a person in serious trouble with no apparent way out, some are encouragement sung to a group of friends, some seem intended primarily as teaching or moral instruction.

It seems (to me) appropriate to make our little psalm about the writing of this book. We need four lines that will form the basic "plot" of our psalm. Here goes:

> Sitting there squinting in Professor Bosma's Old Testament seminary class,
> learning the conventions of Hebrew grammar and poetry . . .
> As assignments go, it wasn't the easiest,
> but so many other things came into focus using those lenses.

Well, that's not going to win any Nobel Prizes, but I do kind of like the structure of it: Two lines setting the scene, then two lines reflecting on its significance; the first and third lines draw you

What Makes Hebrew Poetry Poetic?

into each section by conveying experiences that everyone has had, while the second and fourth lines are less likely to be common experiences. And there's a subtle little chiasm there—the first line's "squinting" is echoed in the last line's "lenses," the middle lines report an "assignment" to be "learned."

I think I'll emphasize that little chiasm by rearranging the words, and while I'm at it I'll tighten things up a bit by deleting some ballast:

> *Squinting in Professor Bosma's class,*
> *the conventions of Hebrew poetry to be learned...*
> *Not my easiest assignment,*
> *yet lenses that brought focus everywhere else.*

In this version, "squinting" and "lenses" come at the beginning of their sentences, "learn" and "assignment" at the end of theirs, to form an elongated X within the poem. And you can see the chiasm more easily, because there's less clutter.

Now let's write the second line for each parallel pair of lines. We should use all four types of parallelism, in the interest of learning about them. Here they are:

- Synonymous (in which the second line is an *echo* of the first)
- Antithetic (the second line gives a *contrast* to the first)
- Synthetic (the second line piles on rich *description*)
- Emblematic (the second line enriches by making a *comparison* to the first)

I'm not sure why these aren't just called "echo," "contrast," "description," and "comparison," but that's out of my hands.

Since the last line of my psalm is sort of a plot twist (and also a climax), fleshing it out with some "synthetic" richer description seems appropriate. Since the second line may not be a common experience for most readers, they might not have a basis to understand a comparison or echo; I'll use antithetic contrast, mentioning some experience that *is* a common one for most people. On the other hand, *everybody* has experienced some difficult assignment,

9

so a synonymous echo probably will work well for that third line, pausing to help people place themselves in the poem through their own life experiences. That leaves an emblematic comparison for line one, and I should use it to help readers place themselves in the classroom with me. (Of course, if you weren't feeling bound to use all four kinds of parallelism in just four lines, you'd be more free to choose which sort of parallelism is best for each section of your poem.)

So we want a psalm that looks like this:

Squinting in Professor Bosma's class,
    (then an emblematic/comparison line)
the conventions of Hebrew poetry to be learned . . .
    (then an antithetic/contrast line)
Not my easiest assignment,
    (then a synonymous/echo line)
yet lenses that brought focus everywhere else
    (then a synthetic/rich description line)

Here's a draft that adds a second line for each phrase:

Squinting in Professor Bosma's class
    (Remember that teacher you loved in that course you couldn't recommend?),
the conventions of Hebrew poetry to be learned,
    like studying the rules of the road, but for truck driving in England.
Not my easiest assignment—
    Never enough time and always too much nuance—
Yet lenses that brought focus everywhere else,
    lifting the veil from the bride, seeing the beauty I'd only heard whispers of.

You can see that I've tried to build in a few flourishes. Line two "breaks the fourth wall" of the scene by directly addressing the readers, to draw them into the action. The second lines in the first three pairs are all mini-parallels of contrasting ideas—love / couldn't recommend, alike / but different, never enough / always too much. Then the punch line *isn't* a contrast, but a double-down description,

What Makes Hebrew Poetry Poetic?

for emphasis: lifting/seeing. That last line about "lenses," in chiasm with the first about "squinting," now gets freighted with lifting a veil and *seeing*. And the mention of "veil" in the last line is a brief *homage* to the Jewish poet Hayim Nahman Bialik's comment that "reading the Bible in translation is like kissing your new bride through a veil."

The very best thing you could do before reading the next chapter would be to write a few psalms for yourself! Try following the pattern I've set out here—writing the first lines of each pair, then filling in the second lines using a type of parallelism that seems appropriate, then trying to tuck in a few pleasant artistic gifts that will help your readers connect with your poem.

To help keep track of those stylistic elements and the other basic building blocks of psalms, you'll find an appendix at the end of this book. Think of it as a field guide to the things that you'll be spotting in the Bible's poetry.

Chapter Two

Selections from Jesus' Prayer Book

IN THIS CHAPTER WE'RE going to settle into the beauty of Hebrew poetry. This will eventually help us settle into the Lord's Prayer. It will also help bring to life much of the beauty of the Hebrew Scriptures.

We'll organize this around the themes that Jesus emphasizes in his prayer. We'll be considering how the Hebrew Scriptures' poetry discusses heaven and earth, kingship and covenant, prophetic teaching and repentance, and priesthood and redemption.

HEAVEN AND EARTH

The Hebrew Scriptures portray human history as the story of an artificial rift that has emerged between heaven and earth.

That's not to say that heaven is a place. When the Bible speaks of God "in the heavens" or the "heavenly Father," it's less a statement about God's *location* than about God's *authority*. The living God, unlike all of the imposters, is not a clever invention of this earth:

> Why should the nations say,
>   "Where is their God?"
> Our God is in the heavens;
>   he does whatever he pleases.

Selections from Jesus' Prayer Book

> Their idols are silver and gold,
> > the work of human hands.
> They have mouths, but do not speak;
> > eyes, but do not see.
> They have ears, but do not hear;
> > noses, but do not smell.
> They have hands, but do not feel;
> > feet, but do not walk;
> they make no sound in their throats.
> Those who make them are like them;
> > so are all who trust in them. (Ps 115:2–8)[1]

"The heavens" represents the domain of God's reign, majesty, authority, and mercy. This realm is not spatially limited, not locked up in some particular location.

Yet we humans *are* creatures of earth, which is indeed a particular location. As the same psalm goes on to say,

> The heavens are the Lord's heavens,
> > but the earth he has given to human beings. (Ps 115:16)

Some of the divine authority was delegated to humans, those in God's image. Humans were made to be priestly mediators between heaven—God's ultimate authority—and this world. The earth was fashioned to be exactly that place for which this delegated human authority would be fitting.

The failure of humans in this priestly role has generated the rift between divine/heavenly authority and the created/earthly order. The Bible is, in a phrase, an account of God's actions to heal this fissure.

In that biblical account, God is portrayed not as a grim destroyer or prim recluse, but as Israel's *savior*. It is not God's intention to annihilate the world that was so well fitted for humans, nor to evacuate them to "heaven." That kind of thinking has more to do with Plato than the Bible. Rather than demolish or abandon

---

1. Parallels include Pss 11, 20, 45, 103; Exod 24; 1 Kgs 22; 2 Chr 6; Jer 23; Lam 3:41; Neh 9; Isa 6, 45, 63, 66; Dan 4, 7; Amos 9; Matt 5:34; 23:22; Heb 8:1.

the creation, God intends to *redeem* it. The Bible's drama portrays God acting to heal the rift between his authority and earth by calling out a particular group of people, through whom God will ultimately bless all people . . . in fact, bless the entire alienated cosmos. In this drama, God promised to ultimately send a new sort of messianic priest who *is* capable of mediating between heaven and earth.

This story line practically shouts from every section of the Hebrew Scriptures. And the writers were so deeply poetic that they can't seem to avoid the conventions of Hebrew poetry, even when they are writing in prose.

For example, consider the chiastic structure of the Pentateuch—the *Torah* or "instruction," the first five books. Every branch of Judaism in Jesus' day accepted *Torah* as divine revelation, the fundamental constitution of their existence as a people. Here is a topical outline of the Pentateuch, where you'll notice how the last book's topics mirror the first book's, the second-to-last mirror those of the second, and the entire chiasm points to the importance of the middle book's topics. That middle book discusses the early stages of healing the rift between heaven and earth, by considering how to live *in God's presence* within the life-giving boundaries of God's instruction:

Prologue: In Genesis 1, a holy sanctuary—the earth—is given life by God's life-giving word, and consecrated by God's presence. Any ancient sanctuary would have been completed by setting up the image of the temple's god; in this story, it is *humankind* at the apex of the story, God's image, commissioned as the priests and caretakers of this sanctuary. Heaven and earth are as they were meant to be—in loving communion with each other.

Selections from Jesus' Prayer Book

Genesis: God's people are expelled from his presence, but a family is gathered. The action's outline, mirrored below in Deuteronomy:
- separation from the nations
- blessing
- seeing the land
- descendants and land

Exodus: God brings his people into his presence—Sanctuary #2 (the tabernacle). The action, mirrored below in Numbers:
- Israel's desert journeys
- apostasy and plagues
- Pharaoh and magicians (mirrored below in Balaam/Balak)
- first-born/Levites

> **Leviticus:** God teaches his people about living in his presence—closing the rift between heaven and earth:
> - cleanliness
> - holiness
> - sacrifices

Numbers: God teaches his people further about living in his presence
- Israel's desert journeys
- apostasy and plagues
- Balak and Balaam
- first born/ Levites

Deuteronomy: God teaches his people yet more about living in his presence
- separation from the nations
- blessing
- seeing the land
- descendants and the land

As if to double down on poetic structure, there's a second set of chiasms running through the themes of these books. This is identified by the use of the Hebrew word *toledoth*, which English translators often (rather unhelpfully) render as "generations." Thus at Genesis 2:4, the first occurrence of *toledoth*, we read: "These are the generations of the heavens and the earth when they were created." Later come the "generations" of Adam, Noah, and others. These passages do sometimes include a genealogy, but that does not seem to be their main point; it would probably be a better translation of the idea involved if we rendered *toledoth* as "the account about" or "the consequences of," or even "now here's the rest of the story concerning the heavens and the earth . . . Adam . . . Noah . . . " It's as if the author is repeatedly answering the question, "Whatever happened to . . . ?"

This "rest of the story" *toledoth* structure runs through the narrative of the Pentateuch. The prologue (Gen 1:1—2:3) gives an introduction in which God is creating the universe, which God called "good," in right fellowship with heaven/God's authority; humans serve as the creation's priests in the presence of God. But something has gone wrong, and beginning at 2:4 we learn what happened to creation as a result of Adam and Eve's response to the divine word. Within the book of Genesis there are two sets of six *toledoth*:

- The first six—Genesis 2:4 (creation), 5:1 (Adam), 6:9 (Noah), 10:1 and 10:32 (Sons of Noah), 11:10 (Shem)—refer to the nations as a whole. This is the story of humanity and its rebellious, disastrous response to God. It is an account of heaven and earth fracturing apart.

- The second six—Genesis 11:27 (Terah), 25:12 (Ishmael), 25:19 (Isaac), 36:1 and 36:9 (Esau), 37:2 (Jacob)—narrow the focus, from "all the families of the earth" and their downward slide, to *one* family through which God will restore things.

These two narratives contrast human-centered action (which is step after step downward into more mayhem) to human dependence on God—step after halting step toward life and a healing of the rift with heaven. For example, you can see this contrast in the way that the first six accounts emphasize humanity's self-sufficient drive toward fruitfulness and multiplication, whereas the last six frequently hover over human barrenness and dependence on God's provision.

This is all a big chiasm, and as you'd expect it "points" to the importance of the event at the center of the chiasm—the call by God of Abraham's family to be his pilot project in the universe.

And that is just the poetic structure *in Genesis!* The *toledoth* pattern continues into the rest of the Pentateuch, where we have . . .

One prologue

Twelve *toledoth* in Genesis, from Eden to Egypt

One *toledoth* of Levites (Exod 6)

Twelve *toledoth* in Numbers 1 (12 tribes), between Egypt and the promised land

One *toledoth* in Numbers 3 (Aaron/Moses, priest and prophet/king of the exodus redemption)

Again, the chiasm "points" to the importance of the idea in the middle: living *in God's presence as God's priests* (which the Levites typify) *of God's creation.*

So both the plot of the Pentateuch and its poetic structure communicate a particular understanding of heaven and earth. Jesus' culture was steeped in that understanding, and we must respect this as we enter into the world of Jesus' prayer. For Jesus' community, this vision of history is not merely an esoteric theory; it is etched in God's practical actions in human history and culture, recorded throughout the Hebrew Scriptures.

One set of historical events particularly typifies this vision of humanity's situation and God's deeds in restoring heaven's relationship with the earth: The redemption brought by God in the events of the exodus. Much in the Hebrew Scriptures reflects back on the events of the exodus, and they are reenacted every year by observing the Passover. The exodus was so foundational to Jesus that he chose the Passover as the narrative for the central act of Christian worship, the distinctive place of Christian fellowship: The Eucharist is the ultimate Passover meal, in which Jesus commemorates the new covenant that prophets had foreseen.

Let's look at two of the psalms that reflect on the engagement of heaven and earth in the exodus.

Psalm 114 gives a condensed vision of the miraculous physical events of the exodus. In an era in which the physical forces of nature were often divinized, the One True God is portrayed as fully in control of nature. He engages all of its potentially frightening faces—floods, earthquakes, winds, and deserts—in making a particular people his dwelling place and sanctuary—that is, in beginning to close the antagonism between earth and heaven.

Psalm 114

(Cf. Exod 14:1–31)

   ¹ When Israel went out from Egypt,
      the house of Jacob from a people of strange language,

    ² Judah became God's sanctuary,
       Israel his dominion.

     ³ The sea looked and fled;
        Jordan turned back.

     ⁴ The mountains skipped like rams,
        the hills like lambs.

     ⁵ Why is it, O sea, that you flee?
        O Jordan, that you turn back?

     ⁶ O mountains, that you skip like rams?
        O hills, like lambs?

    ⁷ Tremble, O earth, at the presence of the LORD,
       at the presence of the God of Jacob,

   ⁸ who turns the rock into a pool of water,
      the flint into a spring of water.

This is one of the many poetic accounts of the exodus in the Hebrew Scriptures (including Exod 15 and Pss 68, 77, 78, 81, 103, 105, and 106). I chose this psalm for our reflection because it is pretty densely packed with conventions of Hebrew poems.

One feature is that every verse is "synonymous" (that is, the second line echoes the first), and also "incomplete": In each pair of lines the first is retold in the second, with one element of the first line left out. This creates the pattern "longer-line—shorter-line"; it would be a "skipping" pattern if you were doing it with your feet. This shortening of the second line is (in the Hebrew) exaggerated in vv. 4 and 6, where "skipping" is mentioned. In the poem there is a whole lot of movement—Israel from Egypt, God toward Israel, the sea and the Jordan fleeing, the mountains moving and the earth trembling, the water springing from rocks—and the poet makes it vivid with a dashing, skipping, tumbling word pattern.

The poem also seems very intent on being a chiasm. I've indented the left margin to help bring this out. Look at the deliberate mirroring of vv. 3–4 in vv. 5–6; these four verses form the "hinge" at the center of the chiasm, persistently asking, "Why does this world seem to be going through convulsions during the exodus?" To underline the mirroring in these four verses, v. 3 and 5 both include a pun (though it's lost in translation), and v. 4 and 6 each have a rhyme in their first line (again, lost in translation).

The chiasm also shows up in the mirrored structure of vv. 1 and 8: Both verses use alliteration, and both are in a 3 + 4 syllable pattern (though, once again, you can't see these things in translation). What *idea* (which *is* visible in translation!) is being reflected between these verses? Israel was led out from a bondage in which they had been "cared for" by slave masters; they were led into a desert where only God could miraculously be their caretaker, and God did not disappoint! Thus the rift between God and God's people is closing. *That* is why the physical world is having convulsions! It is as if a great canyon's walls are being pushed back together.

This is given an exclamation point and explanation in vv. 2 and 7: A group of people has actually become a dwelling place and dominion for the one true God. It is God's own *presence* (the word is repeated twice!) that makes the earth shake. In Eden, humankind's actions banned them from the sphere where they had known intimacy with God—where heaven and earth were properly related. Now God is dramatically acting to begin restoring that relationship and intimacy.

I mentioned that vv. 3 and 5 incorporate a pun. The poet portrays the Red Sea as doing a double-take: It looked, then fled. This literally happens in the account of the exodus, where the waters recede as God's people cross, only to later come crashing back, overwhelming the pursuing forces of Pharaoh with chaos and destruction. This is how God's people were delivered from evil. But the poem points beyond this literal meaning. The Hebrew word for sea, *yam*, is also the name of the Canaanite god of the primordial chaos, of rivers and floods and the raging waters. He is an angry, violent, power-grasping king—how like Pharaoh himself!—described sometimes as "the serpent." So when our poet says that "the *yam* looked and fled," we should not only see the Red Sea turning. All the forces of destruction and enslavement that were arrayed against God's people were, in the end, given a taste of their own medicine, in a demonstration of the supremacy of Israel's God over all the alleged gods of natural forces.

I'd like to briefly look at one more Exodus-themed psalm, Psalm 95, partly because it is widely used in Christian worship, partly because it recounts an event that is echoed in the Lord's Prayer, and partly because it also gives us a concise opportunity to practice appreciating Hebrew poetry.

The poem falls into two sections: a call to worship, followed by a call to obedience. (It is a little sad that the first of these is read in churches so much more frequently than the second!) The call to worship is built around a very condensed retelling of the creation of the universe; the call to obedience is structured around an incident during the exodus.

I'm going to print the English text of the psalm on the left side of the page. On the right side I'll give a running commentary on the poetic conventions in each verse. You might try using your hand to cover the right side of the page, to quiz yourself as you read.

Selections from Jesus' Prayer Book

Psalm 95

¹ O come, let us sing to the Lord; let us make a joyful noise to the rock of our salvation!	synonymous, incomplete
² Let us come into his presence with thanksgiving; let us make a joyful noise to him with songs of praise!	synthetic
³ For the Lord is a great God, and a great King above all gods.	synthetic
⁴ In his hand are the depths of the earth; the heights of the mountains are his also.	synthetic; also a merism: heights + depths = everything
⁵ The sea is his, for he made it, and the dry land, which his hands have formed.	synthetic; another merism
⁶ O come, let us worship and bow down, let us kneel before the Lord, our Maker!	condensed repetition of 1–2; synonymous

⁷ For he is our God,
         and we are the people of his pasture,
         and the sheep of his hand.
	condensed repetition of 3–5; synthetic
	
	 a 3rd line, for emphasis

O that today you would listen to his voice!	1 line / no parallel: Emphatic!!
⁸ Do not harden your hearts, as at Meribah, as on the day at Massah in the wilderness,	synthetic
⁹ when your ancestors tested me, and put me to the proof, though they had seen my work.	synthetic

¹⁰ For forty years I loathed that generation
     and said, "They are a people whose hearts go astray,
     and they do not regard my ways."
	synthetic 3 lines mirror v. 7a;
	
	 v. 7's sheep are wandering

¹¹ Therefore in my anger I swore "They shall not enter my rest."	1 long line mirrors v. 7b *inclusio*: the Voice from 7b speaks

This psalm gives a beautiful call to worship (1–2), then gives a rationale (3–5): The true God has demonstrated his heavenly superiority over all false gods, because he is the creator of the world, whereas they are mere creations of this world. This pattern is repeated, in condensed form, in vv. 6–7, which report the climax of the Genesis 1 creation account in a rather unflattering image: Humans are the sheep of God's pasture. Verses 6–7 so closely parallel vv. 1–5 that you could imagine the two parts being sung responsively by two choirs.

Having stated the awkward truth—people are sheep—the psalm draws a conclusion: sheep really should listen to their shepherd! Do not repeat Israel's great mistake during the exodus, the time of testing at Meribah and Massah.

Meribah and Massah had clearly become watchwords for rebellious, hardened insolence. The place-names were coined by Moses, meaning "quarrel" and "test." God had led Israel to a place at which they became fed up with the manner in which God was providing for them. In this case, water was scarce, and that became the focus of an open rebellion in which Moses was nearly stoned by the people. God replied with an enacted pun: Moses must strike a stone with his staff, the same staff that had been used to strike the Nile and part the Red Sea. From the desert stone, out gushed water.

This incident is reported as an example of God's people putting God "to the test"—putting God on trial. The exodus accounts sometimes speak both of the people putting God to the test, and of God putting the people to the test. God does this as a response when the people are doing it. When the people are rebellious, cheeky, disrespectful, and rude, God sometimes responds by providing an opportunity for them to be stretched into something different.

Psalm 95 cautions that there is a much better way. Having recounted the greatness of God and the waywardness of humanity, the psalmist advises: Listen. Do not rebel. Soften your hearts. Do not drive your hearts astray. You have already seen the goodness of God's works; do not put God to the test, so that there will be no need for God to put you to the test.

Kingship and Covenant

Israel's God is portrayed throughout the Hebrew Scriptures as Israel's true king.

As Psalm 146 puts it,

> Do not put your trust in princes,
>   in mortals, in whom there is no help . . .
> Happy are those whose help is the God of Jacob,
>   whose hope is in the Lord their God,
> who made heaven and earth,
>   the sea, and all that is in them;
> who keeps faith forever;
>   who executes justice for the oppressed;
> who gives food to the hungry.
>   The Lord sets the prisoners free;
> the Lord opens the eyes of the blind.
>   The Lord lifts up those who are bowed down;
> The Lord loves the righteous.
>   The Lord watches over the strangers;
> he upholds the orphan and the widow,
>   but the way of the wicked he brings to ruin.
> The Lord will reign forever,
>   your God, O Zion, for all generations.

You can see that God's kingdom has a particular cast: It is marked by faithfulness, justice, righteousness, and concerned action on behalf of people who are marginalized.

The Bible's emphasis on God as the true king begins on the first page. The literary pattern of Genesis 1 is common enough throughout ancient literature that it is sometimes simply called "the kingship pattern." A great king, confronted with chaos on the borders of the kingdom, rides out to establish order. Upon returning to his capital he builds a structure—often a temple—to commemorate his good rule.

Thus Genesis 1 opens with the description of a formless, dark, deep void. In this case the King is so powerful, so majestic, that he needn't ride out to those chaotic hinterlands; he merely speaks, and things unformed become orderly. The void is filled with life. In the process, God is constructing a magnificent cosmos to commemorate his good rule, a temple in which he will be worshipped. As we've seen, in the end the image of the deity is set up in the temple—in this case, humanity, in God's image, functioning as the priests of this temple. Humans are the intermediaries between God and God's creation, worshipping as they face God, stewarding as they face the creation.

Here's a psalm that follows this kingship pattern, reflects on the Genesis 1 creation account, and ultimately references the messianic King who will come:

PSALM 24
Of David. A Psalm.

¹ The earth is the Lord's and all that is in it, 　the world, and those who live in it;	synonymous
² for he has founded it on the seas, 　and established it on the rivers.	synthetic
³ Who shall ascend the hill of the Lord? 　　And who shall stand in his holy place?	synthetic
⁴ Those who have clean hands and pure hearts, 　　who do not lift up their souls to what is false, 　　and do not swear deceitfully.	antithetic extra "2nd" line, for emphasis
⁵ They will receive blessing from the Lord, 　　and vindication from the God of their salvation.	synthetic
⁶ Such is the company of those who seek him, 　　who seek the face of the God of Jacob. *Selah*	synthetic

Selections from Jesus' Prayer Book

⁷ Lift up your heads, O gates!	synonymous
and be lifted up, O ancient doors!	
that the King of glory may come in.	3rd line: synthetic
⁸ Who is the King of glory?	synthetic
The Lord, strong and mighty,	
the Lord, mighty in battle.	3rd line: synonymous
⁹ Lift up your heads, O gates!	9–10 repeats the 7–8 pattern
and be lifted up, O ancient doors!	
that the King of glory may come in.	
¹⁰ Who is this King of glory?	3+2+2 "broken foot" meter: an intense answer to the recurring question
The Lord of hosts,	
he is the King of glory. *Selah*	

This psalm has a poignant plot: The great king has returned from subduing mayhem (in the act of the creation of the cosmos, vv. 1–2), and is approaching a holy place that commemorates the glory of this work (vv. 7–10). But (vv. 3–6) "Who shall stand in his holy place?" Who can possibly be worthy to accompany him into the temple that commemorates this achievement? Surely such a person must be utterly clean inwardly—hearts and souls, the words on the inside of v. 4—and outwardly—hands and mouths, the words on the outside of v. 4. We imagine ourselves in the crowd, watching the great King ascend toward the holy place, knowing that we do not qualify to join the procession.

This is the basic predicament with which God's people perennially struggled. They are called to be in a special relationship with God that would result in blessing for the entire world. Yet, from the opening pages of Scripture onward, they were living in ways that repeatedly led to disorder and exile from the place to which they had been called. They proved unable to live out their relationship with God, and this set up a pattern: exile from Eden, wandering in a wilderness, a united kingdom that struggled to survive even one century, exile from their own promised land.

One way of thinking about this is to consider the most basic form of the relationship between a great ancient king and the king's people: a covenant. A covenant is a vow between sovereign and subject (often a lesser king), usually involving a list of the blessings of compliance and curses of infidelity. In a covenant, the great king commits himself to the vassals, then the vassals bind themselves to the great king.

The Bible reports a succession of covenants between God and God's people. Noah (Gen 6–9), Abraham (Gen 12, 15, and 17), all of Israel (Exod 19–24 at Sinai, reiterated in Deuteronomy after Israel's unfaithfulness in the desert), and David (2 Sam 7, promising an enduring kingship) are major examples. In every case, the people proved unable to be faithful to the covenant, unworthy to "stand in his holy place."

Yet the Bible's prophecies look forward to a great king who will "stand in" for Israel, fulfilling its covenants with God. And in that day the prophets foresee yet another covenant, a new covenant, that will indeed be fulfilled:

> The days are surely coming, says the Lord, when I will make a new covenant with the house of Israel and the house of Judah. It will not be like the covenant that I made with their ancestors when I took them by the hand to bring them out of the land of Egypt—a covenant that they broke, though I was their husband, says the Lord. But this is the covenant that I will make with the house of Israel after those days, says the Lord:

> I will put my law within them,
>   and I will write it on their hearts;
> and I will be their God,
>   and they shall be my people.
> No longer shall they teach one another,
>   or say to each other, "Know the Lord,"
> for they shall all know me,
>   from the least of them to the greatest,
>   says the Lord;
> for I will forgive their iniquity,
>   and remember their sin no more. (Jer 31:31–34)

Selections from Jesus' Prayer Book

The messianic king would establish this covenant. Hebrew poetry gives rich description of the nature of this messianic reign—the nature of any worthy kingly reign of God's people. This reign will mirror the ultimate reign of the living God, which we encountered in Psalm 146: faithful, just, righteous, an advocate for the marginalized.

These excerpts from Psalm 72 plead for such a reign. Whenever God's kingdom comes, this is what it looks like:

Give the king your justice, O God,	Chiasm: justice
and your righteousness to a king's son.	righteousness
May he judge your people with righteousness,	righteousness
and your poor with justice.	justice
May the mountains yield prosperity for the people,	(Remainder is all synthetic)
and the hills, in righteousness.	
May he defend the cause of the poor of the people,	
give deliverance to the needy,	
and crush the oppressor.	3rd line for emphasis
For he delivers the needy when they call,	
the poor and those who have no helper.	
He has pity on the weak and the needy,	
and saves the lives of the needy.	
From oppression and violence he redeems their life;	
and precious is their blood in his sight.	

Prophetic teaching and repentance

My culture probably overemphasizes the sensational when it thinks of prophets; we reduce "prophecy" to the ability to foretell the future. But this is not a Hebrew prophet's primary vocation. The rift between heaven and earth is rooted in human rebellion, and the prophet's primary duty is to call people back to faithfulness. Thus the primary aim of a prophet is repentance, and the primary tactic of a prophet is teaching.

This is why Deuteronomy looks back on the life of Moses, apparently with the perspective of time, and remarks that no greater *prophet* had since arisen in Israel (34:20), even though you don't see Moses foretelling the future very often. Moses was the conduit of divine instruction. The later prophets follow in that tradition, in Moses' shadow.

So when we look for *prophetic* Hebrew poetry, we should not limit our attention to poetic writing that may be foretelling the future. We should primarily be thinking of poetry that calls God's people back to covenant faithfulness, right relationship with God, and a proper concern for responsible living in God's presence. These are the things that concern prophets.

This prophetic vocation is sometimes expressed as a *concern for God's name*. "God's name" is a reference to God's being, nature, character, and ultimate kingship. So right relationship to God—closing the rift between heaven's authority and earth's ways—is epitomized by reverence for God's name, being, and kingship. Standing at the beginning of all Moses' instruction is the Ten Commandment's first concern—that God's *name* be hallowed. This is the Decalogue's only command that bears an immediate warning. It is not that humans could make God any more holy, but humans can indeed reverence or defame the name, being, and authority of the Holy.

This is why "seeking God's name" is an idiom for repentance (Ps 83:16, for example). In the same way, faithlessness toward the covenant is spoken of as a failure to "hallow" or "sanctify" God's name:

> Thus you shall keep my commandments
> and observe them:
> > I am the Lord.
> You shall not profane my holy name,
> that I may be sanctified among the people of Israel:
> > I am the Lord;
> I sanctify you,
> I who brought you out of the land of Egypt to be your God:
> > I am the Lord. (Lev 22:31–32)

Selections from Jesus' Prayer Book

Consider the following excerpts from a pair of psalms that are built around the idea of God's name. One poem connects God's name to God's heavenly authority; the other pleads that God's people would bless and hallow that name by reverential, covenantal respect.

Psalm 113:1–4, 7–9	Psalm 135:1–4, 19–21
Praise the Lord!	Praise the Lord!
Praise, O servants of the Lord; praise the name of the Lord.	Praise the name of the Lord; give praise, O servants of the Lord, you that stand in the house of the Lord, in the courts of the house of our God.
Blessed be the name of the Lord from this time on and for evermore.	Praise the Lord, for the Lord is good; sing to his name, for he is gracious.
From the rising of the sun to its setting the name of the Lord is to be praised.	For the Lord has chosen Jacob for himself, Israel as his own possession . . .
The Lord is high above all nations, and his glory above the heavens.	O house of Israel, bless the Lord! O house of Aaron, bless the Lord!
He raises the poor from the dust, and lifts the needy from the ash heap, to make them sit with princes, with the princes of his people.	O house of Levi, bless the Lord! You that fear the Lord, bless the Lord!
He gives the barren woman a home, making her the joyous mother of children.	Blessed be the Lord from Zion, he who resides in Jerusalem.
Praise the Lord!	Praise the Lord!

Though the primary work of a prophet like Moses is instruction and exhortation, Moses does indeed sometimes speak of the future. He famously foretold a messianic prophet who would exceed his own work: "The LORD your God will raise up for you a prophet like me from among your own people; you shall heed such a prophet" (Deut 18:15). His use of the word "heed" suggests that this messianic prophet would be a great teacher, and that events would conspire so that his teaching would, at long last, result in covenant faithfulness from the heart. God's name would indeed be hallowed.

Priesthood and redemption

We may also tend to overemphasize the rather sensational work of some priests: their calling to offer sacrifices as they stand between God and God's world, representing each to the other.

But priesthood precedes the Bible's sacrificial system. As soon as the Israelites reach Mount Sinai, before the sacrificial system is introduced, they are told (Exod 19) that by keeping God's instruction and covenant they are "a nation of priests and a holy nation," God's own treasured possession. Long before this, already in Genesis 14, we meet Melchizedek, "priest of God most high," whose work seems to be blessing others with bread and wine; later we are told that Jesus is of the order of *this* priesthood. And, as I've suggested, even in Eden humanity is portrayed as a priesthood within the creation, mediating some of God's authority as they tend the earth, and mediating some of the creation's praise on its return to God.

Thus the priest's primary vocation is covenant faithfulness that blesses the earth and blesses the creator. Priesthood exists in the territory between heaven and earth, able to turn its face toward both God's authority and the creation's potentialities. This was the high original calling of the human race; it preceded the need for prophets to call the people back to faithfulness, and it preceded the emergence of hierarchies that would divide humanity into kings and subjects.

Of course, that original high calling was quickly affected by humanity's response to God. The rift opened between heaven and earth, and the priest's role became more complicated. Now priests must navigate a landscape that has widened into a canyon.

The Bible speaks of this chasm between heaven and earth in many ways, but most fundamentally and frequently the Bible speaks of sin. Sin—the culpable chilling of intimacy with God through rebellion against God—is fundamental to the great rift. So dealing with sin becomes part of the priest's vocation.

Sin is ultimately the irrational, willful rejection of a loving relationship. Because it is irrational, sin requires something more than the instruction of a prophet; because it is willful, sin requires something more than the authority of kingship. Neither of these can restore the love that has been alienated. Sin requires mercy and forgiveness and restoration—it requires a savior, not just a teacher or ruler. And because forgiveness is oriented toward the restoration of a relationship, it generally requires an acknowledgment of the wrong that has been done and a willingness to change, including the willingness to forgive others' sin. Consider Psalm 32:3–5:

> While I kept silence, my body wasted away
> > through my groaning all day long.
> For day and night your hand was heavy upon me;
> > my strength was dried up as by the heat of summer. *Selah*
> Then I acknowledged my sin to you,
> > and I did not hide my iniquity;
> I said, "I will confess my transgressions to the Lord,"
> > and you forgave the guilt of my sin.

Putting it all together

Here is a psalm in which a king considers the interrelationships among kingly authority, prophetic instruction, and priestly forgiveness: I've divided the psalm (using blank lines) into stanzas:

> Psalm 25
> Of David
>
> To you, O Lord, I lift up my soul.
> > O my God, in you I trust;
> do not let me be put to shame;
> > do not let my enemies exult over me.
> Do not let those who wait for you be put to shame;
> > let them be ashamed who are wantonly treacherous.
>
> Make me to know your ways, O Lord;
> > teach me your paths.

Singing with Jesus

Lead me in your truth, and teach me,
    for you are the God of my salvation;
    for you I wait all day long.

Be mindful of your mercy, O Lord, and of your steadfast love,
    for they have been from of old.
Do not remember the sins of my youth or my transgressions;
    according to your steadfast love remember me,
    for your goodness' sake, O Lord!

Good and upright is the Lord;
    therefore he instructs sinners in the way.
He leads the humble in what is right,
    and teaches the humble his way.
All the paths of the Lord are steadfast love and faithfulness,
    for those who keep his covenant and his decrees.

For your name's sake, O Lord,
    pardon my guilt, for it is great.

Who are they that fear the Lord?
    He will teach them the way that they should choose.
They will abide in prosperity,
    and their children shall possess the land.
The friendship of the Lord is for those who fear him,
    and he makes his covenant known to them.
My eyes are ever towards the Lord,
    for he will pluck my feet out of the net.

Turn to me and be gracious to me,
    for I am lonely and afflicted.
Relieve the troubles of my heart,
    and bring me out of my distress.
Consider my affliction and my trouble,
    and forgive all my sins.

Consider how many are my foes,
   and with what violent hatred they hate me.
O guard my life, and deliver me;
   do not let me be put to shame, for I take refuge in you.
May integrity and uprightness preserve me,
   for I wait for you.
Redeem Israel, O God,
   out of all its troubles.

> I've divided the psalm (using blank lines) into stanzas. Each has its own theme, in this order:

> Deliver me, teach me, forgive me (the first three stanzas);
>
>> I praise you, Lord, for your goodness, instruction, love, and faithfulness;
>>
>>> Forgive me
>>
>> I praise you, Lord, for your instruction, deliverance, and friendship;
>
> Deliver and forgive me, and all Israel.

You can feel David sensing that his kingly authority is not enough to win the day. And, though instruction is helpful, he has too often failed to heed it. So he repeatedly returns to his fundamental need for forgiveness and deliverance. His hope is grounded in a restored relationship with God, rooted in God's faithfulness, mercy, and love.

What have we learned about heaven, earth, kingship, covenant, teaching, repentance, priesthood, and redemption? Though earth has become alienated from heaven—God's unique authority, reign, and loving presence—God continues to take action as earth's great redeemer. That action is typified by the exodus, in which bondage to evil gives way to God's personal provision and presence. God, Israel's true king, delivers Israel from evil at the Red Sea, provides for Israel with daily bread in the desert, and leads by cloud and fire; yet God's people test God (and thus must be tested) at Meribah and Massah.

Ultimately, God's redemptive action issues in a forgiveness-working messianic priest who can close the rift between heaven and earth; a messianic prophet whose teaching will bring forth repentance and reverence for God's name; a messianic king who can do God's will and fulfill the terms of Israel's covenants, initiate a kingdom of righteousness and care for the marginalized, and establish a new, enduring covenant.

Heaven, earth, hallowing God's name, God's coming kingdom, fulfilling God's will, daily manna, forgiveness, God's leading, testing in rebellion, deliverance from evil—these are the great themes of the Hebrew Scriptures' poetry, and also the themes of the Lord's Prayer.

Chapter Three

The Prayer of Our Lord

WHICH LORD'S PRAYER?

IT'S NOT VERY PRECISE to speak of *the* Lord's Prayer. The gospels portray Jesus as a person who prays all the time. Luke has a particularly well-developed treatment of prayer, and John gives witness to prayers of Jesus that go on for paragraph after paragraph.

But, nearly from the beginning, Jesus' followers have emphasized a particular prayer for liturgical and devotional use. Perhaps this is because the Lord's Prayer was taught by Jesus in situations where disciples had gathered specifically to be instructed in prayer. The prayer is such a concise, powerful, and beautiful statement of the aims and practice of prayer that there is really no further need to explain its rapid and widespread adoption by the church.

There are two witnesses to this instruction from Jesus about prayer: Matthew 6:9–13 and Luke 11:2–4. Luke's account appears to be an abbreviated version, yet it still includes all of the main elements witnessed by Matthew. Matthew's witness was, by nearly all accounts, written earlier than Luke's, by an author thought to be an eyewitness to the events. Matthew was writing to a Jewish audience, so we might expect readers who were ready for a greater level of detail and a more literal rendition of an Aramaic prayer than Luke's Hellenized readers. (Of course, it is always possible that Matthew and Luke are recording two different events, with Luke describing Jesus as he teaches a more Hellenized group.) Perhaps because of the richness of detail and beauty of form, Matthew's witness has been widely preferred for liturgical purposes.

If we may therefore focus our attention on Matthew's prayer, we still don't quite have a single "Lord's Prayer." Christian practice differs on the use of "debts/debtors" and "trespasses / trespass against." Matthew's *Koine* Greek text uses "debts," though in Jesus' exposition that immediately follows the prayer he uses "trespasses" as a synonym for "debts." Some traditions split the difference and insert Luke's word: "sins." Most English-speaking traditions use "trespasses," for which we may have Origen to thank. Since Jesus seems to have used the words as synonyms, we'll eventually explore the significance of both "debts" and "trespasses."

The best and earliest manuscripts do not include the doxology at the end ("For thine is the kingdom and the power and the glory..."). In contemporary worship the Byzantine Rite does normally include a version of it, as do most Protestants, whose early English translations relied upon a Byzantine text that they, at the time, believed to be more ancient. The doxology is a paraphrase of 1 Chronicles 29:10–13:

> Then David blessed the Lord in the presence of all the assembly; David said:
>
> "Blessed are you, O Lord, the God of our ancestor Israel, for ever and ever.
>
> Yours, O Lord, are the greatness, the power, the glory, the victory, and the majesty;
>
> > for all that is in the heavens and on the earth is yours;
>
> yours is the kingdom, O Lord,
>
> > and you are exalted as head above all.
>
> Riches and honor come from you,
>
> > and you rule over all.
>
> In your hand are power and might;
>
> > and it is in your hand to make great and to give strength to all.
>
> And now, our God, we give thanks to you
>
> > and praise your glorious name."

The Prayer of Our Lord

As a doxology concluding the Lord's Prayer, it appears to have entered the Christian liturgy quite early, probably already in the first century, as it is present already in Didache 8:2.

It is an entirely fitting coda on the rest of the prayer. When David first expresses his interest in building a temple for God (2 Samuel 7), God responds that he will instead build a permanent house *for David*—David will have an heir who will reign perpetually. David's immediate son will be the royal builder of the temple. In 2 Chronicles 29 we hear David praying before God's people, after he has gathered the materials for his son's construction of the temple. David's prayer deeply resonates with the text of the Lord's Prayer, in which Jesus is taking David's place, the fulfillment of the promise of a perpetual Davidic *king*. Jesus is simultaneously portraying himself as the true Temple in which heaven and earth meet, where *priestly* sacrifice is definitively offered. And, of course, Jesus' intent in giving this particular prayer, not unlike David's in 2 Chronicles, is to teach his disciples—part of the messianic *prophet's* teaching vocation. So the doxology ties together the kingly, priestly, and prophetic ministries of the Messiah. All of the themes of the Lord's Prayer find an echo here in 2 Chronicles 29.

Having said that, we will restrict the rest of our work to the text of Jesus' prayer as Matthew bore it witness, without the epilogue from 2 Chronicles.

Some have objected to calling this "the *Lord's* prayer," and prefer "the Disciple's Prayer." Fair enough; the prayer was given as instruction in how disciples should pray. Yet Jesus clearly intends that it would be perpetually prayed with and through *him*, even "in his own name"—that is, as if it were signed by him, conforming to his intentions. This is because prayer is always a participation in something cosmic: It is *in and through Jesus* that the rift between heaven and earth is being healed, and so in and through Jesus that prayer crosses the gap. So we will stay with the prayer's traditional name: the Lord's Prayer.

With these preliminaries out of the way, let's explore how Jesus himself answered the question: How should we pray?

Singing with Jesus

Matthew's Good News

Matthew's gospel has in mind a reader who would deeply resonate with Jewish sensibilities, someone familiar with the Hebrew Scriptures. Matthew is at great pains to portray Jesus as the messianic fulfillment of those Scriptures' promises: An enduring righteous king on David's throne, a prophet who surpasses even Moses, a priest whose sacrifice will finally, successfully close the fissure between heaven and earth. Matthew portrays Jesus as doing all this by successfully reliving the covenants' requirements—requirements at which God's people had failed—and then establishing the new covenant that had been promised.

So Matthew begins with a Jewish genealogy, linking Jesus pointedly to Abraham's covenants, David's kingship, and the Babylonian captivity that resulted from Israel's covenantal failures. The covenants with Abraham and David are about to be fulfilled, and the long captivity of God's people is about to end. The genealogy begins and ends by identifying Jesus as "Messiah"—the fulfillment of the Scriptures' three anointed offices of prophet, priest, and king. "Jesus the Messiah" is then immediately repeated as the narrative commences. Like Isaac, Abraham's son of the covenant, Jesus' conception is miraculous; like Israel, Jesus is forced to live in Egypt; like Moses' generation, Jesus experiences a baptism of entry into Canaan ministry; like Moses receiving the law on Sinai, Jesus spends forty days fasting in the desert; while there he faces temptations that mirror Israel's temptations at Sinai and Eve's temptations in Eden. He calls twelve disciples, as his work will be a fulfillment of the vocation of Israel's twelve tribes. At every turn, Jesus is faithfully living the life to which Israel had been called. And then, in Matthew's fifth chapter, Jesus frames the inauguration of his work by ascending a mountain and giving extended instruction, much as at Sinai Israel paused for months to receive God's instruction during the exodus.

It is in this instruction, Matthew 5–7, that we find Matthew's witness to the Lord's Prayer. Thus the Lord's Prayer's context in the gospel is an event reflecting Israel's exodus from bondage and her pursuit of covenantal intimacy with God.

These three chapters are often called "the Sermon on the Mount," but it is likely that this was not a simple half-hour sermon. One commentator has called these chapters "the syllabus on the mount"; the text is probably, in abbreviated form, a summary of instruction and training that went on for some time, perhaps months.

We'll not be exploring the later sections of Matthew's gospel, but the themes I've introduced here do continue throughout the gospel. Matthew portrays Jesus as the Messiah who faithfully lives out Israel's covenants: Jesus is the Christ, demonstrating the nature of his kingdom, conveying his prophetic teaching, and offering his priestly sacrifice for sin.

Jesus the psalm-writing preacher

Once you're familiar with Hebrew poetry, you begin to notice how prominent it is in Scripture. For example, look at Jesus' first words of instruction on the mountain, a beautiful example of Hebrew parallelism:

> Blessed are the poor in spirit,
>   for theirs is the kingdom of heaven.
> Blessed are those who mourn,
>   for they will be comforted.
> Blessed are the meek,
>   for they will inherit the earth.
> Blessed are those who hunger and thirst for righteousness,
>   for they will be filled.
> Blessed are the merciful,
>   for they will receive mercy.
> Blessed are the pure in heart,
>   for they will see God.
> Blessed are the peacemakers,
>   for they will be called children of God.

Blessed are those who are persecuted for righteousness' sake,
> for theirs is the kingdom of heaven.

Blessed are you when people revile you
and persecute you
and utter all kinds of evil against you falsely on my account.
> Rejoice and be glad,
>> for your reward is great in heaven,
>> for in the same way they persecuted the prophets who were before you.

The first eight of these nine sayings have a lock-step form ("Blessed are [attribute], for they will [result]"). This block of eight begins and ends with an *inclusio* ("for theirs is the kingdom of heaven"), which would normally indicate the beginning and end of a section of text. The eight sayings' verb tenses form a chiasm (present, future passive, future transitive, future passive, then the same in reverse order). Some scholars also believe that there is a theme in the first four that may be contrasted to a theme in the last four.

From this structure in the first eight sayings you would not expect to see a ninth. It is an explosive exposition of the eighth saying, in rather graphic detail. This poetic structure makes a point: each verse teaches that eventually good will triumph but, as the ninth verse makes abundantly clear, this project is definitely not going to be easy on Jesus' followers.

It's not that persecution is a good thing in itself, something that people should seek out so that God will owe them a blessing. Consider instead the structure of the entire sermon: It begins with this poem, which emphasizes the *external* challenge of rejection by others because of *faithful* behavior; it ends with an extended discussion of the *internal* challenge of our chronic *unfaithful* behavior. These two challenges frame all of the sermon's instruction on piety and discipleship. For many of us—certainly for me—our death grip on our idols is only pried open by some combination of difficult external hardships and significant internal moral failures.

The Prayer of Our Lord

These are the things that force us to acknowledge the depth of our need, and so these constitute the hard and narrow road of discipleship. Such is our natural hostility to heaven.

The rest of this long "sermon" is structured in this poetic way:

- Jesus gives commentary on five of the themes of the great commandments: murder, adultery, swearing falsely, taking vengeance, loving enemies.
- Then come three sections on practicing piety: almsgiving, prayer, and fasting.
- Then we're back to commentary on five more themes: greed, lust, unfaithfulness, anxiety, harsh criticism.
- Finally come three more elements of practicing piety: Don't throw pearls to swine, do pray, do exhibit compassionate integrity.

So we have ten "commandments," interspersed with threefold discussions of piety. Prayer comes up at the center of each section about piety; prayer is central to actually practicing all of the things in this sermon. Some have even argued that the entire sermon is patterned after the Lord's Prayer.

Now let's focus on the section of this sermon in which Jesus teaches the Lord's Prayer. It consists of an introduction (in which Jesus describes how *not* to pray), the prayer, and a short epilogue (in which Jesus, as if underlining and italicizing, emphasizes the importance of forgiving others).

The Introduction

The introduction to the prayer is usually typeset as simple prose, in a paragraph. But just a little mindful indenting helps clarify the structure of parallelism in these introductory comments. (The epilogue about forgiving is also given in the poetry of parallelism, as we'll see.) I've labelled the flow of logic as IA, IB, IIA, and IIB; there are two main sections (I and II), each with a negative warning (A) about bad behavior and a positive exhortation (B) about behaving differently.

IA. And whenever you pray, do not be like the hypocrites;
> for they love to stand and pray in the synagogues and at the street corners,
>> so that they may be seen by others.

Truly I tell you, they have received their reward.
> IB. But whenever you pray,
>> go into your room and shut the door and pray to your Father who is in secret;
>>> and your Father who sees in secret will reward you.

IIA. When you are praying, do not heap up empty phrases as the Gentiles do;
> for they think that they will be heard
>> because of their many words.
>>> IIB. Do not be like them,
>>>> for your Father knows what you need
>>>>> before you ask him.

You can see that there is a tremendous amount of echoing in these stanzas:

- And whenever you pray ... But whenever you pray ... When you are praying
- Do not be like the hypocrites ... do not heap up empty phrases as the Gentiles do ... Do not be like them
- For they love to stand ... for they think that they will be heard
- Pray in the synagogues and at the street corners ... go into your room and shut the door
- Because of their many words ... before you ask him
- So that they may be seen by others ... your Father who sees in secret
- They have received their reward ... will reward you
- Father who is in secret ... Father knows what you need

I think that this echoing is deliberate. The sort of "prayer" Jesus describes here is not directed to the living God; it is prayer in an echo chamber . . . prayer spoken, ultimately, to ourselves.

In deeply poetic form, Jesus is asking his followers to consider whom they are addressing in prayer. God is not a judge on a live-performance TV show—"If I can just get my performance right and impress him, I'll get what I want." God is not a genie—"If I can just get the right formula, I'll be heard." And prayer is not a market transaction—"If I heap up enough words (or feelings or deeds) I'll be successful." Instead . . . "Pray then in this way," says Jesus, and then immediately begins the Lord's prayer by addressing God as *Father*. Jesus shows how to pray if you're praying *to God*, a loving Father who already knows what you need and therefore doesn't require a long list of petitions for favors.

We've been saying all along that the meaning of writing is conveyed, in part, by its genre and form. As you may be expecting by now, the prayer that follows this preamble is in the form of a chiastic Hebrew poem. Each stanza is a group of (usually two) parallel lines.

The Lord's Prayer

To sink into the Lord's Prayer, I think it will be helpful to see its form from Matthew in his *Koine* Greek.[1] On the right, I've given a literalistic rendering of each word's meaning. I have also included in parentheses some ideas that are implied by a word's case or voice. This isn't really a translation, but I think that knowing the placement of the words in the text can be helpful:

---

1. Instead of reporting the Greek letters, I've transliterated the prayer into English characters. I've used ē to represent η and ō to represent Ω. Here ō rhymes with "so" (just like in English) i rhymes with "see" (like in the Spanish *si*), ei and ē both sound the same and rhyme with "weigh" and "né," and o and a both sound the same and rhyme with "Tom" and "saw."

Pater hēmōn,	Father ours,
ho en tois ouranois:	*the (Father) in the heavens:*
Hagiasthētō to onoma sou,	May revered* (be) the name yours,
elthetō hē basileia sou,	may come the kingdom yours,
genēthētō to thelēma sou,	may be done the will yours,
Hōs en ouranō kai epi gēs.	*as in heaven also on earth.*
Ton arton hēmōn ton epiousion	The bread ours the daily
dos hēmin sēmeron,	*give us today,*
kai aphes hēmin ta opheilēmata hēmōn	and forgive (to) us the debts ours
hōs kai hēmeis aphēkamen	*as also we forgive the debtors ours,*
tois opheiletais hēmōn,	
kai mē eisenenkēs hēmas eis peirasmon	and (may you) not lead us into testing
alla hrusai hēmas apo tou ponērou.	*but rescue us from the evil.*

* that is, honored as holy; hallowed

As will be obvious by now, this prayer is in the form of a five-part chiastic psalm. The first four of the five stanzas are "synthetic," building up rich description; the last is an antithetic, contrasting verse.

Verse-by-Verse Analysis

Let's first take a brief look at some details in each of these psalm stanzas.

1. Father ours, the (Father) in the heavens:

These are extremely short lines, among the shortest to be found in Hebrew poetry. What a brilliant way to draw a contrast to the babblers who heap up words!

As we've seen, referring to God as "in the heavens" is a statement of God's authority, not God's location. So the prayer opens by combining the intimacy of fatherhood with the grandeur of the living, true God who makes, directs, and loves all things.

The Prayer of Our Lord

There's not a verb in these lines, so you might think of them as a "vocative" form of address—just as there's no verb when you write "Dear dad" at the start of a letter.

We also should note that this prayer's pronouns are plural, not singular, when they refer to those doing the praying. Especially in the West we are likely to pray this prayer as if it said "my Father . . . show me your will for my life . . . give me bread . . . forgive me . . . deliver me from evil." That isn't incorrect, but it is incomplete. The focus of this prayer is on the community, not the individual. "May the community of Jesus' followers honor God by its collective presence and reputation in the world . . . may God provide food for our hungry fellow travelers . . . may the Christian tradition be forgiven its grievous missteps, as it consistently shows public grace to others . . . may the church, as a community, be delivered from unfaithfulness and persecution."

2. May honored as holy the name yours, may come the kingdom yours,
   may be done the will yours, as in heaven also on earth.

The first thing you notice about this stanza is that, compared to other psalm stanzas we've seen, it is elongated and inverted. Usually the pattern is a single line, followed by one (or sometimes two, or rarely three) related lines. Here it's one line plus three lines, and the trio comes first, not last.

This is not accidental. Matthew's gospel opens with the question all of Palestine was asking: *Who is the true king?* Is it Augustus? Herod? The kingdom of the magi? What about God's kingship? When will God's reign finally be made evident? Matthew addresses these questions by making the kingdom of heaven one of his major themes. Throughout the gospel Matthew draws a distinction between the surrounding kingdoms and the kingdom of heaven, by witnessing to Jesus' extended teaching on the topic. That teaching consistently shows that Jesus' kingdom, like the Psalms' description of the righteous king's reign, is an inverted kingdom: The first become last, the leaders are the servants of all, the outcasts are welcomed in, the sick are made well, sinners are forgiven, children are honored, the rich are cast down, the etiquette of patronage is renounced while the tax collectors and prostitutes take a place in the kingdom of heaven. Other kings vie for power in a zero-sum game, but in Jesus' kingdom all the nations are blessed.

So it's poetic justice that this stanza about God's kingdom would be elongated for emphasis, and inverted for consistency: Jesus' kingdom is an upside-down kingdom. This is the nature of the kingdom of heaven, the reign that is apparent when the rift between heaven and earth closes—as the prayer puts it, "on earth, as it is in heaven."

We who pray this prayer in English are apt to split up the three lines that form the beginning of this stanza. I think most of us even take a breath after "hallowed be your name," as if there's a paragraph break there. Maybe that's because the next two lines almost rhyme in English ("... kingdom come, ... will be done"), and so they seem separated from "hallowed be thy name." But when you look at Matthew's Greek you can see that the three lines belong together as a block: They have the same length, the same ordering of parts of speech, the same third-person-imperative verb form, and a great deal of assonance among the vowel sounds (first words all end in ētō, third words end in -a, all three lines rhyme).

And the first and third lines definitely want to stay together: There's a mirrored *inclusio* in the middle of the first and third lines: "—thētō to *ono*ma sou...—thētō to *thele*ma sou." And there's mirroring in the passive voice of the first and third lines' verbs, sandwiching line #2's active verb between them. For these reasons, you might say that the three lines form a miniature chiasm, which points to "thy kingdom come" in the middle as the theme of three parallel concepts—God's name, kingdom, and will. People who pray this prayer are seeking to align with God's character, reign, and intentions for the world. They are begging to be a part of the new covenant, in which God's Spirit so fills God's people that they readily obey from the heart. And they are blessing God, asking God to continue to bring honor to his name, his authority, and his good aims for the creation.

The closing "on earth as in heaven" mirrors the opening "Father in heaven," an *inclusio* that draws to a close this section of the prayer.

3. The bread ours the daily give us today.

The *Koine* word rendered as "daily" in this sentence is a *hapax legomenon*—a word that does not occur anywhere else in ancient literature, not even in the classical literature that preceded *Koine* Greek. So far as we know, Jesus coined this word. This makes translation somewhat difficult, because we lack a broad context about how the word was used. It appears to be a compound word, referring to something that is coming upon us. Scholars have suggested "daily," "this day," "the coming day."

You'll have noticed that, as prayers go, the Lord's Prayer does very little asking for *stuff*. It does not even ask for good health, a very common prayer in the ancient world. This short stanza is the only phrase that requests anything you might call stuff-like. For that reason, some commentators sweep in a great number of personal requests as legitimate extensions of this stanza. I'll have more to say about that, and about the indeterminacy of our *hapax legomenon*, in just a moment.

4. And forgive (to) us the debts ours as also we forgive the debtors ours.

Debts? Transgressions? Sins? The Greek word in the prayer generally means debt or obligation, yet in the verses (Matthew 6:14–15) immediately following the prayer Jesus uses the word "transgression" as a synonym, as if giving commentary on his own prayer:

And forgive us our debts,
    as we also have forgiven our debtors . . .
For if you forgive others their trespasses,
    your heavenly Father will also forgive you;
but if you do not forgive others,
    neither will your Father forgive your trespasses.

Singing with Jesus

Perhaps "debts" was chosen as the word to be used in the prayer (and then immediately clarified by "trespasses" after the prayer) partly because the Greek "debt" word's root (*aphe* . . .) has such great assonance with the word for forgiveness (*ophe* . . .). Their pronunciation is identical. Try saying the Greek version of this stanza out loud a few times—I'll write it phonetically, vowels short unless marked:

	Kī	afes	hāmin	ta	afălāmata	hāmōn
Hōs	Kī	hāmās	afăkamen	tois	afăletās	hāmōn

That feels like something between hip-hop lyrics and a Gilbert & Sullivan tongue twister. Sounds are mirrored within each line: afes . . . afălāmata, hāmin . . . hāmōn in line 1, hāmās . . . hāmōn, afăkamen . . . afăletās in line 2. And all of the sounds of the first line are directly mirrored in the words of the second, with a nice juxtaposition near the beginning (afes . . . afăkamen, hāmin . . . hāmās). Children always love things like this, and you can imagine centuries of *Koine*-speaking kids all around the Mediterranean looking forward to reciting this stanza at night-time prayers.

Mentioning "debt" also is a gentle reminder to Jesus' followers of the exodus-Sinai instruction about observing a year-long sabbatical (every seven years) and a sabbatical-of-sabbaticals year (the Jubilee, every 7 x 7 years). In those years debts were set to expire, along with indentured servitude. Here in Matthew Jesus is beginning his public ministry with a reference to the sabbatical-year instruction, just as he does in Luke's gospel by reading from Isaiah 61:

> The Spirit of the Lord is upon me,
>   because he has anointed me
>   to bring good news to the poor.
>
> He has sent me to proclaim release to the captives
>   and recovery of sight to the blind,
>
> to let the oppressed go free,
>   to proclaim the year of the Lord's favor.

The sabbatical laws provided for any kinsman-redeemer to step up and institute the provisions of the law at his or her own expense. This is how Jesus represents his ministry at its inauguration; he is here to see that debts which cannot be repaid are forgiven and indentured servants redeemed. When you read "debt" in the context of the clarification about "transgressions," the notion of a *moral* debt or servitude clearly seems to be in play. Again, more on this in just a moment.

    5. And not lead us into testing, but rescue us from (the) evil.

The first phrase's last word might be rendered "testing," as in an examination to find the actual nature of something, or rendered "temptation," as when seeking to make someone fail. It's been pointed out that it would be odd to suggest that God could lead people into *temptations*, when the prayer has just begged that God's character and kingdom would be made manifest. In a moment I'll give more reasons to favoring "testing" as a translation rather than "temptation."

Many have made something of the definite article that precedes "evil," insisting that the prayer is invoking *personalized* evil—"the evil one." This would be consistent with the apparent meaning of the same phrase at Matthew 5:37, 13:19, and 13:38. Some modern translations have therefore rendered this verse as something like "Save us in the time of testing, and rescue us from the evil one." In just a moment we'll have more to say about this, too.

The Imagery of the Psalm

We've seen that Matthew has been portraying Jesus as the new Moses who is preaching in a situation that mirrors Sinai, giving an exposition of Sinai's law. So we might be expecting that this prayer, like some other psalms we've investigated, will draw its imagery from the exodus. Consider these parallels:

Singing with Jesus

1. Our Father in heaven

As we've seen, to say that God is in heaven is to say that this God is the one and only God, who rules all things. This was the fundamental affirmation underlying the exodus. God's people must be allowed to depart from Egypt's polytheism and worship the one true God. The plagues demonstrate, in grim succession, the true God's superiority over the alternative pantheon. This invocation of God's name is an affirmation that there is only one God, and all others are idol pretenders.

2. Hallowed be thy name, thy kingdom come, thy will be done, on earth as it is in heaven.

Throughout the exodus accounts, particularly in Leviticus, the disobedience of God's people—the failure to do God's will—is depicted as profaning or tarnishing God's name, the special covenant name given at the outset of the exodus narrative. Disobedience publicly dishonors God's character, causing God's kingship as the true Ruler of the universe to not be recognized. Thus a prayer that God's name be hallowed is a prayer that God's people might be found faithfully doing God's will, and that God might come to be seen for what God is—the true King, the Name above all names.

Throughout the exodus account, the fracture between earth and heaven is being addressed. For example, the instructions for the tabernacle are presented as a replication or model of true heavenly things; the tabernacle then becomes a place on earth filled by God's own glory. By asking "on earth as it is in heaven," this prayer asks that all of life might begin to conform to this pattern of intimacy between God and God's creation.

3. Give us our bread for today/tomorrow

You'll remember that this phrase involves a *hapax legomenon*. So far as we know, Jesus made up a word that might mean "today" and might mean "tomorrow." Since the prayer is invoking exodus imagery, you can see the brilliance of this invention: This stanza refers to manna in the wilderness, which was given fresh every day . . . except on Friday, when people collected bread both for today and for tomorrow, so that the Sabbath might be observed. Manna was a way of teaching complete dependence on God's provision.

So this phrase of the Lord's Prayer is concisely teaching several things: God's people are declaring complete dependence on God's provision; they are affirming that they will accept as a blessing whatever form that provision takes, and live in contentment; and they are affirming their need for Sabbath rest, yet another way of expressing complete dependence on God's provision.

In the exodus account, the people's attitude toward manna emerges as the great barometer of the entire nation's respect for God, and therefore an indicator of their health in the covenants. For example, hear Deuteronomy 8:3

> He humbled you by letting you hunger,
>> then by feeding you with manna,
>> with which neither you nor your ancestors were acquainted,
> in order to make you understand
>> that one does not live by bread alone,
>> but by every word that comes from the mouth of the Lord.

How appropriate that manna would appear at the center of the chiastic Lord's Prayer, with the rest of the prayer's elements pointing toward it.

4. Forgive us our sins, as we forgive those who have sinned against us

As we've seen, "sins" has been translated as both "debts" and "trespasses." In the context of exodus imagery, both metaphors for sin make sense.

The entire exodus narrative is the story of redemption from debt. God's people were slaves, completely owned by / indebted to forces that were resisting God's will. Those in slavery could not possibly pay their own way out of their indebted situation. God had to act miraculously to redeem them out of bondage.

And, after liberation, flippancy toward God is portrayed as trespassing a boundary. For example, the people are warned to not come too close to Sinai, as a metaphor for all presumptive sin:

sin is always the crossing of a good boundary, a transgression into space where life will not flourish. The *Torah's* instruction is, put negatively, a "no trespassing" sign marking out territory that is unconducive to life.

Redemption and forgiveness are, of course, not ends in themselves. This stanza is not just a plea for a "get out of jail" card. Forgiveness and redemption are always in the service of restoring a relationship—in this case, of healing the fracture between God and God's creation, and restoring an active, loving, trusting relationship with God.

5. Lead us not into testing; deliver us from the evil one

We've seen that testing is something that figured prominently in the exodus, and that God's examination of the people is a response to their rebellious testing of God. The Bible's archetype of this phenomenon is the experience at Massah and Meribah. God was of course actively *leading* the people—by cloud and pillar of fire—and at Massah and Meribah the people rebel against the way in which God is leading and providing for them. As a result of the people's testing of God, they were led to a place of testing.

The exodus is also one long account of deliverance from evil and an Evil One, personified by Pharoah. The Bible's poetry celebrates one particular event as an archetype of this long deliverance: The miraculous safe crossing of the Red Sea, and the chilling defeat of Pharaoh's pursuing army. Consider Psalm 106:9-12, for example:

> He rebuked the Red Sea, and it became dry;
> > he led them through the deep as through a desert.
> So he saved them from the hand of the foe,
> > and delivered them from the hand of the enemy.
> The waters covered their adversaries;
> > not one of them was left.
> Then they believed his words;
> > they sang his praise.

There is a long Christian tradition of tying this hymn of deliverance from Pharaoh to the work of Christ in delivering God's people from evil. As St. John Paul II put it in his May 2, 2001, general audience:

> It is not by chance, in the solemn Easter Vigil, that every year the liturgy makes us repeat the hymn sung by the Israelites in Exodus. That path which was opened for them, prophetically announced the new way that the risen Christ inaugurated for humanity on the holy night of his resurrection from the dead. Our symbolic passing through the waters of Baptism enables us to relive a similar experience of passing from death to life, thanks to the victory over death won by Jesus, for the benefit of us all.

One might therefore paraphrase this section of the Lord's Prayer in this way: "We do not ever want to rebel against God's care to the point where God must test us to reclaim us; instead, please miraculously intervene so that our temptations, and evil itself, die under your hand." Jesus is the great covenant-keeper, and this prayer is a plea from his followers that they might receive a share in his decisive fulfillment of the covenants and victory over the forces of evil.

Cumulatively, these references to the exodus desert experiences make a point: Following Jesus will be a humbling experience of utter dependence upon God as a wilderness is traversed, rather than a triumphal conquest of a promised land. Jesus' contemporaries expected a Messiah of the triumphal sort. Surely, they thought, this is the moment when the secularizing forces will be driven out, and God's law will become the law of the land? No, surely not. Jesus' disciples perpetually misunderstood this point; they seem, right up until the ascension, to be dreaming of a conquest in which they would seize political power so that their vision of God's will would be done. This has been one of the perennial weaknesses of Jesus' followers throughout the centuries.

The Structure of the Psalm

This prayer's topics come in two bundles.

The first six lines approach God, and pursue the theme of closing the rift between heaven and earth. They do this by speaking three blessings. The praying believer affirms that her focus is not on her own reputation, reign, or will, but God's.

The other six lines make three requests: provisions for one more day, grace for everyone, protection from sin and evil. If the first six lines emphasize the fullness of heaven, the second six lines acknowledge the neediness of earth.

This is all arranged in a chiasm, tying the two bundles together: The first and last two lines, when combined, affirm that because God is our mighty father we can trust God for deliverance. The second and fourth pairs of lines affirm that because God's kingdom is our greatest good, we should confess where we have rebelled against it, and actively align ourselves with it. The stanza at the middle—the hinge of the chiasm—acknowledges that we depend on God *for everything*, and will be content with and thankful for the manna he sends.

The Meaning of the Psalm

If one wanted to tie up all of these considerations into a paraphrase of the prayer, it might look like this:

> Our Father of all majesty, only true God,
> > Bring yourself honor; let us be your obedient children as your reign is made evident.
> > > Each moment we depend on your provision, in gratitude and contentment.
> > We depend on your forgiveness, and in gratitude forgive those who wrong us.
> > Keep us lovingly content with your care, and please defeat the evil that threatens us.

But, seriously, the point of this little book was *your* delight in Hebrew poetry as a genre. So why not take a moment to jot down your own paraphrase of the Lord's Prayer?

Appendix

Field Guide to Hebrew Poetry

1. **Parallelism:** This is the basic structure of most Hebrew poetry. It consists of groups (usually pairs) of statements that relate to each other, stacked together into a poem. There are four common ways in which these pairs of statements are related:

   a. Synonymous (*echo* lines—each thought of the first line is repeated in the second). As a rare triple example, consider Psalm 1:1:

   > Happy are those
   > *who do not follow the advice of the wicked,*
   > *or take the path that sinners tread,*
   > *or sit in the seat of scoffers*

   b. Synthetic (the second line adds *description*). For example, keep reading Psalm 1, vv. 2–3:

   > But their delight is in the law of the Lord,
   > *and on his law they meditate day and night.*
   > They are like trees planted by streams of water,
   > *which yield their fruit in its season,*
   > *and their leaves do not wither.*
   > *In all that they do, they prosper.*

Appendix

c. Emblematic (the second line makes a *comparison*; often the first line is literal, the second metaphoric or simile). Keep at it: Psalm 1:4:

> The wicked are not so,
> *but are like chaff that the wind drives away.*

d. Antithetic (the second line is in *contrast* to the first). Psalm 1:6:

> For the Lord watches over the way of the righteous,
> *but the way of the wicked will perish.*

These are often mixed within the poem (as here in Psalm 1), though sometimes one type of parallelism is repeated for a climactic effect. That seems to be Habakkuk's approach in this passage that my wife and I read at our wedding. This is also an example of Hebrew poetry in a prophetic book, outside the Psalms:

> Though the fig tree does not blossom,
>   and no fruit is on the vines;
> though the produce of the olive fails,
>   and the fields yield no food;
> though the flock is cut off from the fold,
>   and there is no herd in the stalls,
> yet I will rejoice in the Lord;
>   *I will exult in the God of my salvation.*
> (Hab 3:17–18)

Parallelism can be "complete" or "incomplete." That is, sometimes each of the second line's parts corresponds to one of the first line's parts, and other times some words are strategically omitted for effect. Notice here how the psalmist has made the parallelism in the first (synonymous/echo) phrase incomplete (omitting "of the Lord"), so that there will be mirror-like parallelism with the other (synthetic) two lines:

> One thing I asked of the Lord,
>> that will I seek after:
> to live in the house of the Lord
>> all the days of my life,
> to behold the beauty of the Lord,
>> and to inquire in his temple. *(Ps 27:4)*

When the parallelism is "incomplete" there is sometimes "compensation"; the poet adds words to take the place of those that were deleted, so we have the same number of units in each line, but the units do not convey identical meanings.

> For the LORD is a great God,
>> And a great King above all gods. *(Ps 95:3)*

"Great God" and "great King" parallel each other; the omission of "the LORD" is compensated by "above all gods."

In addition to our four types of parallelism, some analysts have identified *climactic* parallelism (the second line adds a summarizing phrase), though distinguishing this from an echo or a rich description seems difficult to me. You could also recognize *external* parallelism in places—where there is a form of parallelism *across* the line-pairs of the poem, not just within them. Here's an example:

> Zion shall be redeemed by justice,
>> and those in her who repent, by righteousness.
> But rebels and sinners shall be destroyed together,
>> and those who forsake the Lord shall be consumed.
>> *(Isa 1:27–28)*

The second line adds description to the first (technically that's synthetic incomplete parallelism with compensation!), and the fourth line does the same service to the third line. But when you compare the first *two* lines to the last *two* lines, the "external" parallelism is antithetic; the second pair stand in contrast to the first pair.

Appendix

2. **Stylistic elements that are usually visible in the English translation:**

   a. *Chiasm*: The "sense units" are repeated, in inverted order. This is usually conveyed symbolically in this way: A, B, C, D, . . . , D', C' B', A'.
   b. *Inclusio*: Repetition of an idea or word at the beginning and end of a passage. This appears to have been, among other things, a way of identifying section breaks in ancient documents that were copied by hand. The author could not be confident that copyists would reproduce the physical arrangement of the words on the page, so sections were marked with an *inclusio* rather than something like indenting.

Psalm 118 is a nice example. It remarkably contains antiphonal call-and-response praise, an extended personal testimony, a praise song within a praise song, and a number of oft-quoted keynote phrases: "The stone that the builders rejected has become the chief cornerstone . . . This is the day that the Lord has made; let us rejoice and be glad in it . . . Blessed is the one who comes in the name of the Lord." And around these elements the psalmist places the *inclusio* of (identical) vv. 1 and 29, bookends that place all the rest in a particular context:

> O give thanks to the Lord, for he is good;
> *his steadfast love endures forever!*

   c. *Merismus*: Two extreme parts are used to represent an entirety. Psalm 139, for example, uses several merisms to communicate the exhaustive nature of God's being and knowledge:

> O Lord, you have searched me and known me.
> You know **when I sit down and when I rise up**;
>   you discern my thoughts from far away.
> You search out **my path and my lying down**,
>   and are acquainted with all my ways . . .

> If I **ascend to heaven**, you are there;
>> if I **make my bed in Sheol**, you are there . . .
>
> If I say, "Surely the **darkness** shall cover me,
>> and the **light** around me become night," . . .

The psalmist's point is not that God only sees when we are sitting or beginning to stand, or only in heaven and Sheol. The merisms' meaning is that God knows and sees all, everywhere, at all times.

> d. Piling up synonyms: This often draws attention to the thing being described, as in Psalm 119's many different words for *Torah*. Here are the first seven verses, with the synonyms in **bold**:
>
>> Happy are those whose way is blameless,
>>> who walk in the **law** of the Lord.
>>
>> Happy are those who keep his **decrees**,
>>> who seek him with their whole heart,
>>
>> who also do no wrong,
>>> but walk in his **ways**.
>>
>> You have **commanded** your **precepts**
>>> to be kept diligently.
>>
>> O that my ways may be steadfast
>>> in keeping your **statutes**!
>>
>> Then I shall not be put to shame,
>>> having my eyes fixed on all your **commandments**.
>>
>> I will praise you with an upright heart,
>>> when I learn your righteous **ordinances**.

3. **Stylistic elements that are often not visible in the English translation** (though you should still use them when writing your own psalms!):

    a. Syndetic vs. Asyndetic: Hebrew *prose* is often *syndetic*; that is, each phrase of the narrative begins with the equivalent of "and." When the "and" is missing from a line, that is meant to draw our attention to something.

Appendix

But Hebrew *poetry* is usually *asyndetic*. This means that if you're reading a poem and see a string of lines beginning with "and," that word has been repeatedly used for a reason. Usually this is a way of saying "you need to pay attention to every single line here!"—a way of interrupting the pattern of parallelism, to give weight to each line on its own grounds.

Translators, always eager to "help," sometimes obscure this meaning when they translate. Probably they think it might seem odd and redundant to an English speaker if each line started with "and . . . " But it can be an important signal in Hebrew poetry when, unlike the usual parallelism, every line stands on its own.

Consider these syndetic lines that open Isaiah 5. You can imagine the prophet solemnly looking you right in the eye, every line a punch line:

> My beloved had a vineyard
> on a very fertile hill.
> He dug it and cleared it of stones,
> and planted it with choice vines;
> he built a watch-tower in the midst of it,
> and hewed out a wine vat in it;
> he expected it to yield grapes,
> but it yielded wild grapes.

b. Assonance/Alliteration: Assonance is the repetition of a vowel sound (". . . so old it is that no man knows . . . ," "Would that he took a look at this book, and he should."). Alliteration is the repetition of an initial sound ("Peter Piper picked . . . ").

c. Acrostic: When each verse begins with a letter of the alphabet in sequence. Psalms 25, 34, 37, 111, 112, 119, and 145 are acrostics; also Proverbs 31:10–31.

d. Rhythms: Though Hebrew poetry is known for its parallelism more than measured meter, meters matter. A 3 + 3 pattern of syllables is common. A 3 + 2 pattern can indicate lament, and in general long-line-followed-by-short-line is sometimes thought to be dirge-like. A 2 + 2 + 2 pattern, as will be apparent if you use it in a poem, indicates urgency.

These can be mixed. Finishing a string of common-pattern lines with a single out-of-pattern line gets one's attention, as with the 3 + 3 + 3 + 3 + ... + 3 + 2 "broken foot" meter, often taken to signal intensity

  e. Wordplay: Just as meters matter, ...

- Rhymes sometimes occur.
- So do "turns," the repetition of a root across different words, as in "his head was headed on the wrong heading."
- Likewise root-play, transposing the letters of a word root—"Did you hear the hare?"
- Also puns: using words with multiple meanings—"I used to be a tap dancer until I fell in the sink"—or sound-alikes with different meanings—"Being vegan is a missed steak."
- And paronomasia—two words that sound alike, as in "Champagne for my real friends and real pain for my sham friends." Or even "meters matter."
- And don't forget anadiplosis: repeating, at the start of a line, the phrase from the end of the prior line. Here's an example from Psalm 133, where it seems especially appropriate in a "psalm of ascent," sung as you pull up one foot after the other while you climb the hills toward Jerusalem:

> How very good and pleasant it is when kindred live together in unity!
> It is like the precious oil on the head running down upon the beard,
>   on the beard of Aaron,
>   running down over the collar of his robes.

Appendix

- Finally, a close relative of anadiplosis: breaking up common word pairs across lines. This is a nice way of shaking people up, directing their attention to things that have become too familiar by repetition. You hear this in hip-hop poetry as well.

www.ingramcontent.com/pod-product-compliance
Lightning Source LLC
Chambersburg PA
CBHW051705090426
42736CB00013B/2548